THE WORLD OF
PETER RABBIT
POSTCARD BOOK

TM

30 CARDS

With new reproductions from the original illustrations by

BEATRIX POTTER

F. WARNE & Co

FREDERICK WARNE

Published by the Penguin Group
27 Wrights Lane, London W8 5TZ, England
Viking Penguin Inc., 40 West 23rd Street, New York, New York 10010, USA
Penguin Books Australia Ltd, Ringwood, Victoria, Australia
Penguin Books Canada Ltd, 2801 John Street, Markham, Ontario, Canada L3R 1B4
Penguin Books (NZ) Ltd, 182-190 Wairau Road, Auckland 10, New Zealand

Penguin Books Ltd, Registered Offices: Harmondsworth, Middlesex, England

First published 1990
1 3 5 7 9 10 8 6 4 2

ISBN 0 7232 3647 X

Printed and bound in Singapore by Imago Publishing Limited

INTRODUCTION

Beatrix Potter's delicate watercolour illustrations for her famous Tales are beautiful paintings in their own right. She drew from life and many of her landscapes and backgrounds can still be recognized today while her animal characters are always essentially naturalistic, even when clothed. Beatrix filled pages of her sketchbooks with studies of all kinds of animals in characteristic poses and then used these sketches as reference for the finished watercolours for the books. Her passion for accuracy was such that she even spent an entire afternoon in a pigsty making studies for *The Tale of Pigling Bland*, and many of her best-loved characters were real animals whom she kept as pets – Peter and Benjamin, Mrs. Tiggy-winkle the hedgehog 'who *did* bite' when she got tired of modelling, Hunca Munca the mouse who sadly died after a fall from the chandelier.

The first of the little books, *The Tale of Peter Rabbit*, started life as a story letter to Beatrix's friend, five-year-old Noel Moore (the son of Annie Moore, at one time Beatrix's governess) in 1893. Peter Rabbit was eventually published as a book in 1902 and proved so popular that in the next ten years another fifteen books were published, although the last of the 23 Tales – *The Tale of Little Pig Robinson* – did not appear until 1930.

Although she was always rather reserved and shy, and in old age rather crusty on occasion too, Beatrix Potter understood and liked children, in particular the young Moores, later the younger members of the Warne family, and later still the many readers of her little books who wrote to her. For them she developed the imaginary world of the Tales with delightful letters, some of them charming miniature letters in tiny envelopes purporting to be from the animals themselves. 'Sir,' writes Squirrel Nutkin to Old Brown the Owl, 'I should esteem it a favour if you would let me have back my tail, as I miss it very much. I would pay postage.' There is a very funny series of letters about Mrs. Tiggy-winkle's deficiencies as a washerwoman, and Peter Rabbit even planned another raid on Mr. McGregor's garden by post!

Beatrix Potter was a prolific correspondent on a wide variety of subjects all her life, and also designed greetings cards for commercial publishers and charities such as ICAA. These beautiful postcards are an appropriate reminder of this most entertaining of letter writers.

POSTCARD

POSTCARD

'One table-spoonful to be taken at bed-time.'
Reproduced from an original unpublished
watercolour by Beatrix Potter for *The Tale of
Peter Rabbit*
© Frederick Warne & Co., 1955

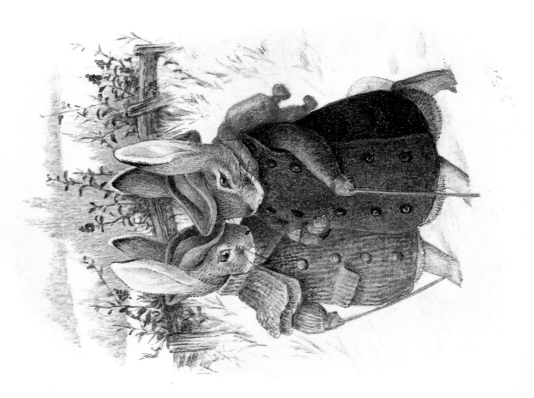

POSTCARD

POSTCARD

POSTCARD

POSTCARD

POSTCARD

POSTCARD

POSTCARD

Cecily Parsley brewing cider
Reproduced from an unpublished watercolour by
Beatrix Potter for *Cecily Parsley's Nursery Rhymes*
© Frederick Warne & Co., 1987

POSTCARD

'We love our little garden,
And tend it with such care,
You will not find a faded leaf
Or blighted blossom there.'
Reproduced from an original watercolour by
Beatrix Potter for *Cecily Parsley's Nursery Rhymes*
© Frederick Warne & Co., 1922, 1987

POSTCARD

'You know the old woman
who lived in a shoe?
And had so many children
she didn't know what to do?'
Reproduced from an original watercolour by
Beatrix Potter for *Appley Dapply's Nursery Rhymes*
© Frederick Warne & Co., 1917, 1987

POSTCARD

'He picked a bunch of primroses and tied them up
with a bit of darning-wool that Aunt Dorcas had
given him.'
Reproduced from an original watercolour by
Beatrix Potter for *The Tale of Little Pig Robinson*
© Frederick Warne & Co., 1930, 1987

POSTCARD

'The counter inside was a convenient height for
rabbits.'
Reproduced from an original watercolour by
Beatrix Potter for *The Tale of Ginger and Pickles*
© Frederick Warne & Co., 1909, 1987

POSTCARD

'Butter and milk from the farm.'
Reproduced from an original watercolour by
Beatrix Potter for the frontispiece of *The Tale of
The Pie and The Patty-Pan*
© Frederick Warne & Co., 1905, 1987

POSTCARD

"'Oh! Mother, Mother,' said Moppet, "there's
been an old woman rat in the kitchen, and she's
stolen some of the dough!'"
Reproduced from an original watercolour by
Beatrix Potter for *The Tale of Samuel Whiskers*
© Frederick Warne & Co., 1908, 1987

POSTCARD

POSTCARD

POSTCARD

'One place suits one person, another place suits
another person. For my part I prefer to live in the
country, like Timmy Willie.'
Reproduced from an original watercolour by
Beatrix Potter for *The Tale of Johnny Town-Mouse*
© Frederick Warne & Co., 1918, 1987

POSTCARD

'And now Timmy and Goody Tiptoes keep their
nut-store fastened up with a little padlock.'
Reproduced from an original watercolour by
Beatrix Potter for *The Tale of Timmy Tiptoes*
© Frederick Warne & Co., 1911, 1987

POSTCARD

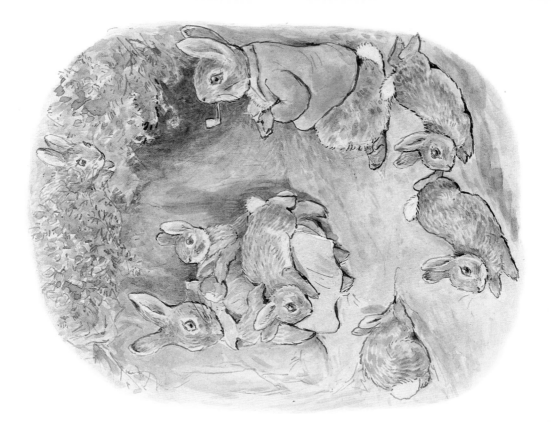

POSTCARD

'When Benjamin Bunny grew up, he married his
Cousin Flopsy. They had a large family, and they
were very improvident and cheerful.'
Reproduced from an original watercolour by
Beatrix Potter for *The Tale of The Flopsy Bunnies*
© Frederick Warne & Co., 1909, 1987

POSTCARD

'"But as to a nest – there is no difficulty: I have a
sackful of feathers in my woodshed," said the
bushy long-tailed gentleman.'
Reproduced from an original watercolour by
Beatrix Potter for *The Tale of Jemima Puddle-Duck*
© Frederick Warne & Co., 1908, 1987

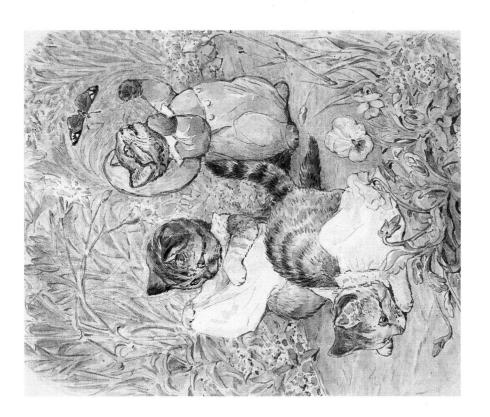

POSTCARD

'Moppet and Mittens walked down the garden
path unsteadily. Presently they trod upon their
pinafores and fell on their noses. When they stood
up there were several green smears!'
Reproduced from an original watercolour by
Beatrix Potter for *The Tale of Tom Kitten*
© Frederick Warne & Co., 1907, 1987

POSTCARD

'The boat was round and green, and very like the
other lily-leaves.'
Reproduced from an original watercolour by
Beatrix Potter for *The Tale of Mr. Jeremy Fisher*
© Frederick Warne & Co., 1906, 1987

POSTCARD

'Hunca Munca has got the cradle, and some of
Lucinda's clothes.'
Reproduced from an original watercolour by
Beatrix Potter for *The Tale of Two Bad Mice*
© Frederick Warne & Co., 1904, 1987

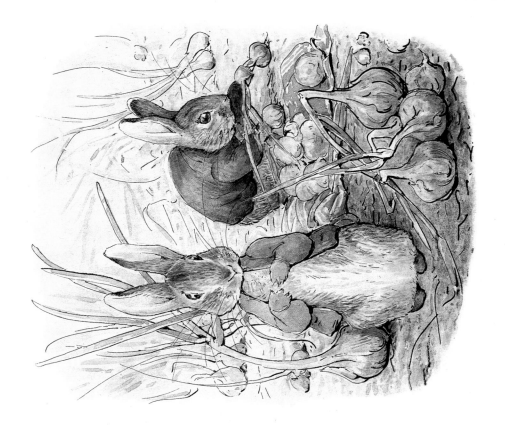

POSTCARD

POSTCARD

'In the tailor's shop in Westgate Street the
embroidered silk and satin lay cut out upon the
table – one-and-twenty button-holes – and who
should come to sew them, when the window was
barred, and the door was fast locked?'
Reproduced from an original watercolour by
Beatrix Potter for *The Tailor of Gloucester*
© Frederick Warne & Co., 1903, 1987

POSTCARD

'The squirrels filled their little sacks with nuts,
and sailed away home in the evening.'
Reproduced from an original watercolour by
Beatrix Potter for *The Tale of Squirrel Nutkin*
© Frederick Warne & Co., 1903, 1987

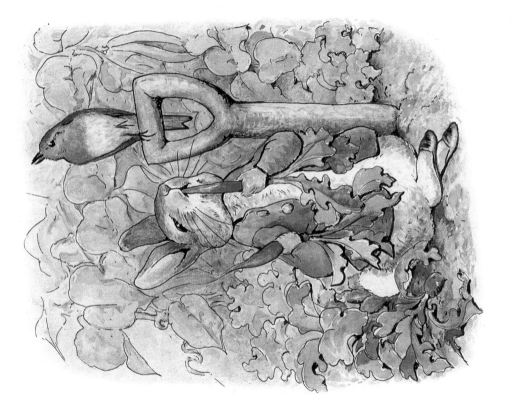

POSTCARD